New York Real Estate Broker Exam

"You never fail until you stop trying" - Albert Einstein

For inquiries;
info@xmprep.com

Unauthorised copying of any part of this test is illegal.

New York Real Estate Broker Exam #1

Test Taking Tips

☐ Take a deep breath and relax

☐ Read directions carefully

☐ Read the questions thoroughly

☐ Make sure you understand what is being asked

☐ Go over all of the choices before you answer

☐ Paraphrase the question

☐ Eliminate the options you know are wrong

☐ Check your work

☐ Think positively and do your best

Table of Contents

SECTION 1	
DIRECTION	1
PRACTICE TEST	2 - 15
ANSWER KEY	16
SECTION 2	
DIRECTION	17
PRACTICE TEST	18 - 30
ANSWER KEY	31
SECTION 3	
DIRECTION	32
PRACTICE TEST	33 - 46
ANSWER KEY	47
SECTION 4	
DIRECTION	48
PRACTICE TEST	49 - 61
ANSWER KEY	62
SECTION 5	
DIRECTION	63
PRACTICE TEST	64 - 75
ANSWER KEY	76
SECTION 6	
DIRECTION	77
PRACTICE TEST	78 - 89
ANSWER KEY	90

Copyright © Educational Testing Group, All rights reserved.
This booklet may not be reproduced and transmitted in any form by any means without the permission of the publisher.
This booklet has been prepared and printed in USA.

TEST DIRECTION

DIRECTIONS

Read the questions carefully and then choose the ONE best answer to each question.

Be sure to allocate your time carefully so you are able to complete the entire test within the testing session. You may go back and review your answers at any time.

You may use any available space in your test booklet for scratch work.

Questions in this booklet are not actual test questions but they are the samples for commonly asked questions.

This test aims to cover all topics which may appear on the actual test. However some topics may not be covered.

Studying this booklet will be preparing you for the actual test. It will not guarantee improving your test score but it will help you pass your exam on the first attempt.

Some useful tips for answering multiple choice questions;

- Start with the questions that you can easily answer.

- Underline the keywords in the question.

- Be sure to read all the choices given.

- Watch for keywords such as NOT, always, only, all, never, completely.

- Do not forget to answer every question.

Special assessment designates a unique charge in which government units can assess against real estate parcels for specific public projects.

Who pays special assessment?

A) Only those property owners that will experience a benefit from the assessment
B) All property owners in the community
C) All residents of the community
D) None of the above

In an assignment, which of the following is the original tenant responsible of?

A) The assignee
B) The landlord
C) The managing agent
D) No one

Homeowner's insurance refers to a type of property insurance which covers losses and damages to an individual's house and assets in the home.

Which of the following is not covered by a standard coverage homeowner policy?

A) Flood
B) Fire
C) Theft
D) Vandalism

Which of the following items given below is not a necessary element of a contract?

A) Meeting of the minds
B) Earnest money
C) Competent parties
D) Consideration

5

A **percolation test** refers to a test that determines the water absorption rate of soil in preparation for the building of a septic drain field or infiltration basin.

Which of the following people administers the percolation test?

A) Department of Buildings
B) Department of Health
C) Tax assessor
D) Building inspector

6

A **capital improvement** refers to the addition of a permanent structural change or the restoration of a property that will either enhance the property's overall value and increase its useful life or adapt it to a new use.

What cost is considered to be a capital improvement rather than an expense?

A) Roof repair
B) Salesperson commission
C) A for-sale sign on the property
D) Addition of a two-car garage

7

A broker must subordinate his or her personal interests to which of the following personnel?

A) Client
B) Customer
C) Sales agent
D) Third party

8

Which of the following does a mortgage broker need to disclose to a loan applicant?

A) The number of lenders that will be solicited by the broker
B) The application fees
C) The conditions for fee refunds
D) All of the above

9

Real estate appraisal describes the process of creating an opinion of value for real property.

Which of the following is determined in a property first by a tax assessor like a real estate appraiser?

A) Mortgage value
B) Market value
C) Insured value
D) Assessed value

10

Which of the following is the document whereby a purchaser of a property personally obligates herself to the lender?

A) Deed
B) Mortgage
C) Covenant
D) Power of Attorney

11

Which of the following organizations may impose liability for clean up of real estate contaminated by toxic substances?

A) NHPA
B) NEPA
C) CERCLA
D) None of the answers are correct.

12

Which of the following is the result of the death of a landlord?

A) Automatic renewal of the lease
B) Indefinite extension of the lease
C) Termination of the lease
D) Cheers and cartwheels

13

All building tenants use meeting spaces, lobbies, restrooms and other amenities in which landlords also charge for the use of these spaces.

Which of the following is the basis of an office-building tenant in paying rent?

A) Viable square feet
B) Usable square feet
C) Carpetable square feet
D) Rentable square feet

14

The right of redemption is the legal right of any mortgagor who owns real estate to reclaim his or her property. After you lose your home at a foreclosure sale, you might be able to get the property back because the right of redemption allows you to get your home back before or after a foreclosure.

Which of the following refers to redemption before a foreclosure sale and a redemption after a foreclosure sale, respectively?

A) Statutory, Equitable
B) Equitable, Statutory
C) Judicial, Nonjudicial
D) Civil, Equitable

15

For which of the following losses does liability insurance protect the insured?

A) Injuries and damage to people
B) Fire
C) Windstorm
D) All of the above

16

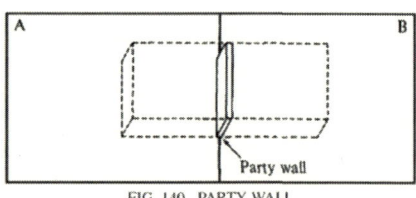

FIG. 140. PARTY WALL

A **party wall** is a wall that is common in two adjoining rooms.

A party wall is an example of which of the following?

A) Appurtenance
B) Easement
C) Encroachment
D) Incoherent

CONTINUE ▶

17

Lien refers to the official order allowing someone to keep a person's property who owes them money until there is full payment.

Which of the following determines the priority of a lien?

A) Date of the court hearing
B) Date of making the lien
C) Date of paying off the lien
D) Date of recording the lien

18

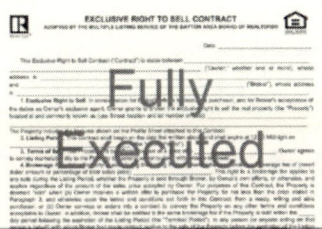

Which of the following refers to an executed contract?

A) It is not yet fully signed
B) It is fully signed
C) It is not yet fully completed
D) It is fully completed

19

An **asset base** is the underlying assets that give value to a company, investment or loan.

Which of the following refers to a basis whereby an asset is depreciated at the same amount in each accounting period?

A) Short-term basis
B) Deductible basis
C) Straight line basis
D) None of the above

20

Two sisters, Mia and Isabella, own a property as joint tenants. Isabella decides to sell her share to a third person for a reduced amount.

Which of the following is the correct way to address the third person upon closing?

A) Joint tenant with Mia
B) Tenant in common with Mia
C) Tenant by the entirety with Mia
D) Tenant at will with Mia

21

In investing, the **cash-on-cash return** refers to the ratio of annual before-tax cash flow to the total cash invested amount in percentage that is widely used to evaluate the cash flow from income-producing assets.

Which of the following is the cash on cash return of an investment having a $45,000 cash flow and a cash investment of $250,000?

A) 17%
B) 18%
C) 19%
D) 20%

22

A **quitclaim deed** refers to an instrument used in transferring interest in real property.

Which of the following is the use of quitclaim deed?

A) To transfer property from an estate to a heir
B) To foreclose on a property by a lender
C) To restore mining rights
D) To remove a cloud on the title

23

Usury became common first in England under the rule of King Henry VIII.

Which of the following most accurately describes usury?

A) It is the illegal use of another's property
B) Charging fees for borrowing money
C) Charging an illegally high interest rate for borrowed funds
D) It is the illegal use of another's money

24

Which of the following happens if passive losses of a taxpayer exceeds the allowable limit for that year?

A) The allowable limit goes up the same amount the following year.
B) The loss may be carried over to a future year when the taxpayer meets passive activity limit loss rules.
C) The lost passive is gone which can only be used in the specified tax year.
D) The taxpayer will be penalized about 10% for the over the limit amount.

CONTINUE ▶

25

Market value should exchange on the date of valuation between a willing buyer and a willing seller in an arms-length transaction after proper marketing wherein the parties had each acted knowledgeably and prudently.

Which of the following percentages of market value must be insured for a replacement cost to be in effect?

A) 80%
B) 75%
C) 25%
D) 20%

26

Easements are rights given to a person or entity to trespass upon or use land owned by somebody else. Landlocked homeowners sometimes pay for an easement to cross the land of another to reach their home.

Which of the following creates an easement in gross?

A) Current owner
B) Former owner
C) Sheriff
D) Utility company

27

The **right of survivorship** is a characteristic of several types of joint ownership of property. When jointly owned, the property includes a right of survivorship and so the surviving owner automatically absorbs the dying owner's share of the property.

Which of the following does the right of survivorship apply to?

A) Life tenants
B) Joint Tenants
C) Holdover tenants
D) Tenants in common

28

Asbestos contains any of the several minerals (such as chrysotile) that readily separate into long flexible fibers, which cause asbestosis. Asbestosis have been implicated as causes of certain cancers. For many years it has been used as a fireproof insulating material in buildings.

Which of the following can only remove asbestos if it is subject to federal and state asbestos regulations?

A) Licensed and bonded cleaning business
B) Licensed asbestos remover companies
C) The homeowner acting alone
D) General Contractor

29

Property valuation refers to the process of developing an opinion of value for real property.

Which of the following is true regarding the effects of income and expenses on property valuation?

A) Capital expenses have no effect on property value.
B) Higher profit means higher property value.
C) Lower profit means higher property value.
D) Profit has no effect on the property value.

30

An **equalization factor** is used as a multiplier to assess the value of a property to get a value for the property that is in line with statewide tax assessments.

When is an equalization factor needed?

A) When senior citizens are deserving of a lower tax rate.
B) When a major company contributes most of the community's tax revenue.
C) When multiple communities contribute to a regional high school.
D) When commercial and residential properties need to be taxed at different tax rates.

31

Which of the following is the rate for taxpayers if a taxpayer has a tax bracket of 28%?

A) 5%
B) 10%
C) 15%
D) 20%

32

A house flipper renovates a kitchen in a city which adopts the ICC model codes.

Which of the following building codes is the flipper most concerned about in his kitchen renovation?

A) International Building Code
B) International Existing Building Code
C) International Residential Code
D) None of the answers are correct.

33

The **Fair Housing Act** bans the refusal to rent or sell a dwelling to any person because of race, color, religion, sex, familial status, or national origin.

Which of the following groups does the Federal Fair Housing Act of 1968 apply to?

A) Only those states that do not have state fair housing laws
B) Only people in the 15 southeastern states of the United States
C) Landlords and homeowners only
D) None of the above

34

Housing discrimination is when an individual or a family is treated unequally when trying to buy, rent, lease, sell or finance a home based on specific characteristics, such as race, class, sex, religion, national origin, and familial status.

If there is an incident of discrimination, which of the following does the complainant need only to prove?

A) The act caused a loss.
B) The act was in a pattern of discrimination.
C) The act was intentional.
D) Discrimination occurred.

35

Which of the following is true of a Real Estate Investment Trust?

A) Each investor owns a specific property in the trust.
B) REIT's can only be sold when a property is sold.
C) The trust can only have one type of underlying investment.
D) Shareholders receive profits from rent or mortgage payments.

36

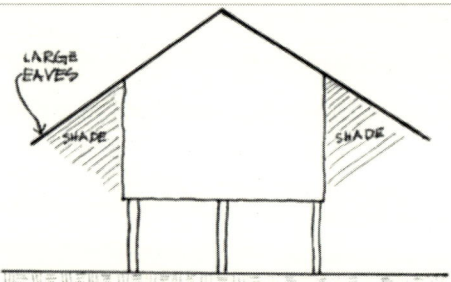

Which of the following describes the eaves of a structure in the portions of the roof?

A) Comes together at the peak
B) Allows the attic spaces to breathe
C) Overhangs from the sides
D) None of the above

37

Property tax is an assessed real estate tax which is usually based on the value of the property owned and is often evaluated by local or municipal governments. It is a primary source of revenue for many local governments.

Which of the following about property tax is not correct?

A) It is a real estate ad-valorem tax, calculated by a local government, which is paid by the owner of the property.
B) It is usually based on the value of the owned property, including land.
C) Millage rate is the other name given to property tax.
D) Property classes, tax rates, assessment rules and valuations are constant and do not vary by jurisdiction.

38

"Jurisdiction in rem" describes the exercise of power by a court over property or a "status" against a person over whom the court does not have in personam jurisdiction.

An in-rem procedure is against which of the following?

A) Retail business owner
B) Property owner
C) Property
D) Municipal government

39

A **Multiple Listing Service** (MLS) is a type of service used by a group of real estate brokers. They band together to create an MLS that allows each of them to see one another's listings of properties for sale.

Which of the following should a licensee immediately call upon obtaining a written offer on an MLS property?

A) MLS
B) The listing broker
C) The property owner
D) None of the above

40

A married couple decides to list their house for sale. The Husband meets with a Real Estate Representative and tells him that he and his wife would give her the listing. Husband signs the listing agreement.

Which of the following is the status of the listing agreement?

A) Void because all the owners of a property must sign on their listing agreements.
B) Valid because because it simply gives the broker the right to market the property.
C) It is illegal
D) Unenforceable

41

In which of the following scenarios should the state mandated disclosure statement be presented to prospective clients?

A) At the first substantive meeting
B) When there is a meeting of the minds
C) When the transaction goes into contract
D) Only if the client buys or sells a property through the broker

42

Are Your Radon Levels Safe?

Radon is known as a naturally occurring radioactive gas which comes from the radioactive decay of uranium. It is usually found in igneous rock and soil, but in some cases, well water may also be a source of radon.

Which of the following is true for radon gas?

A) It is colorless
B) It is harmful
C) It is odorless
D) All of the above

43

Tax assessment determines the value, and sometimes, the use of a property to calculate a property tax.

Which of the following is the first step in contesting a property's tax assessment?

A) To meet with the mayor
B) To meet with the building inspector
C) To meet with the tax assessor
D) To meet with the tax collector

44

The **payoff statement** reflects the remaining loan balance, the number of payments and the rate of interest. It also states the amount of interest that will be rebated due to prepayment by the borrower.

Which of the following refers to paying off a loan by making installment payments?

A) Amortization
B) Habendum
C) Satisfaction
D) Usury

45

A **Building Permit** is a type of authorization that is required by a government or other regulatory body and it must be granted before the construction of a new or existing building can legally occur.

Which of the following is the purpose of a building permit?

A) Ensuring that the sanitary conditions for septic systems are met
B) Ensuring that the community is developing in accordance with the master plan
C) Ensuring that the building facades are culturally correct
D) None of the above

46

Which of the following should an appraiser not consider in performing an area-regional and neighborhood analysis of residential property?

A) Whether the area has a high level of conformity
B) Whether the property is located in a desirable school district
C) Whether the local economy has a variety of employment opportunities
D) Whether the area has a high ratio of real estate agents to mortgage brokers

47

Good Faith Estimate refers to an estimate of fees that is due at closing for a mortgage loan which must be provided by a lender to a borrower.

Which of the following is the number of business days which a loan applicant must receive a good faith estimate?

A) Three
B) Seven
C) Ten
D) Thirty

48

Which of the following describes recapture of depreciation?

A) The federal government forcing elderly property owners into the street
B) The state government seizing property from an unpopular person
C) The federal government recovering sheltered taxes after the sale of an investment property
D) A municipality fining property owners for unsatisfactory property maintenance

SECTION 1

#	Answer	Topic	Subtopic	#	Answer	Topic	Subtopic	#	Answer	Topic	Subtopic	#	Answer	Topic	Subtopic
1	A	TC	SC3	13	D	TA	SA1	25	A	TC	SC2	37	D	TC	SC1
2	D	TD	SD5	14	B	TD	SD7	26	D	TA	SA7	38	C	TC	SC3
3	A	TC	SC2	15	A	TC	SC2	27	B	TA	SA2	39	B	TB	SB5
4	B	TD	SD5	16	B	TA	SA2	28	B	TD	SD1	40	B	TB	SB5
5	B	TB	SB6	17	D	TA	SA2	29	B	TA	SA3	41	A	TB	SB4
6	D	TC	SC1	18	D	TD	SD5	30	C	TC	SC3	42	D	TD	SD1
7	A	TB	SB4	19	C	TC	SC1	31	C	TC	SC1	43	C	TB	SB6
8	D	TA	SA4	20	B	TB	SB4	32	B	TB	SB3	44	A	TA	SA7
9	B	TC	SC3	21	B	TA	SA1	33	D	TB	SB2	45	B	TB	SB6
10	C	TA	SA7	22	D	TD	SD2	34	D	TB	SB2	46	D	TA	SA7
11	C	TB	SB3	23	C	TA	SA7	35	D	TD	SD4	47	A	TD	SD2
12	C	TD	SD5	24	B	TD	SD4	36	C	TD	SD1	48	C	TC	SC1

Topics & Subtopics

Code	Description	Code	Description
SA1	Commercial Investment	SC2	Property Insurance
SA2	Estates & Interests	SC3	Taxes Assessment
SA3	Income Approach to Real Estate Valuation	SD1	Construction & Environmental Issues
SA4	Mortgage Brokerage	SD2	Deeds & Title Closing Costs
SA7	Real Estate Market	SD4	Real Estate Investment & Analysis
SB2	Human Rights & Fair Housing	SD5	The contract of sales and leases
SB3	Land Use & Regulations	SD7	Forms of Property Ownership
SB4	Law of Agency	TA	Economics
SB5	License Law	TB	Rules & Regulations
SB6	Municipal Agencies	TC	Taxes & Insurance
SC1	Income Tax Issues	TD	Transactions & Processes

TEST DIRECTION

DIRECTIONS

Read the questions carefully and then choose the ONE best answer to each question.

Be sure to allocate your time carefully so you are able to complete the entire test within the testing session. You may go back and review your answers at any time.

You may use any available space in your test booklet for scratch work.

Questions in this booklet are not actual test questions but they are the samples for commonly asked questions.

This test aims to cover all topics which may appear on the actual test. However some topics may not be covered.

Studying this booklet will be preparing you for the actual test. It will not guarantee improving your test score but it will help you pass your exam on the first attempt.

Some useful tips for answering multiple choice questions;

- Start with the questions that you can easily answer.

- Underline the keywords in the question.

- Be sure to read all the choices given.

- Watch for keywords such as NOT, always, only, all, never, completely.

- Do not forget to answer every question.

1

Deed restrictions refer to private agreements restricting the use of the real estate and are listed in the deed. The seller may add a restriction to the title of the property.

Which of the following makes the deed restriction invalid when its right has been restricted?

A) Installing a swimming pool
B) Raising horses
C) Growing crops
D) Selling the property

2

For which of the following expenses should an investment property seller be able to give accurate figures?

A) Property taxes
B) Finance costs
C) Insurance
D) All of these answers are correct.

3

Which of the following does a loan originator use to determine the estimated value of a property based on an analytical comparison of similar property sales?

A) An appraisal
B) An area survey
C) A market survey
D) A cost-benefit analysis

4

The **Civil Rights Act of 1866** explains citizenship and affirms that the law equally protects all citizens.

Which of the following refers to the basis for the Civil Rights Act of 1866 that prohibits discrimination without exception?

A) National Origin
B) Race
C) Religion
D) All of the above

5

Which of the following can be the best source to determine the legally recognizable location and boundaries of a parcel of real estate?

A) City map
B) GIS mapping site on the Internet
C) Legal description in a deed
D) Post office

CONTINUE ▶

6

Functional obsolescence refers to a reduction of an object's usefulness or desirability because of an outdated design feature that cannot be easily changed.

Which of the following would be the most likely example of functional obsolescence?

A) An entirely pink tile bathroom floor with a matching countertop and a shower surround
B) A change in zoning is permitting mixed use when it was just a residential zone before
C) The building of a stadium across the highway
D) The presence of nearby housing

7

Net operating income or NOI refers to a calculation used to analyze real estate investment generating income.

To determine net operating income, from which of the following are the expenses deducted?

A) Gross income
B) Variable income
C) Vacancy factor
D) Cash flow

8

Which of the following refers to a rule or regulation passed by a local government, such as a city?

A) Code
B) Law
C) Ordinance
D) Statute

9

A **sales agent** sells or distributes products in a given territory but he is self-employed, takes title to the goods, and does not act as agent for a principal.

Which of the following may compensate a sales agent?

A) The buyer
B) His own broker
C) Another sales agent
D) The seller

10

An **operating expense** refers to the ongoing cost for running a business, system or product.

Which of the following expenses are not included in calculating net operating expenses?

A) Property Taxes
B) Property Insurance
C) Utility Charges
D) Mortgage Interest

11

Tacking refers to a legal concept arising under a common law relating to competing priorities between two or more security interests arising over the same asset.

Which of the following defines the process of tacking?

A) Adding successive time periods for owners and former owners to acquire an easement
B) Establishing a lien on a property through a court action
C) Filing a lis pendens with the county clerk
D) None of the above

12

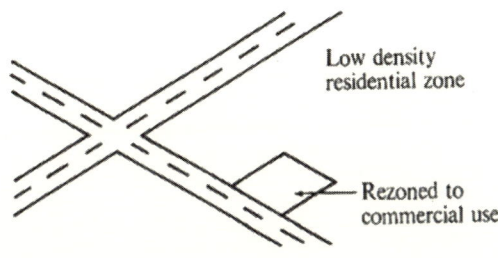

Which of the following best refers to spot zoning?

A) Used to control the number of people living in a zone
B) Used primarily to bring new businesses to an area
C) Used to bring property values in line with neighboring parcels of property
D) A use for land that serves a useful purpose to neighborhood residents

13

A **security deposit** refers to the deposit money to the landlord to assure the payment of rent and other responsibilities of the lease performed.

Which of the following would the security deposit the lessor has on hand for a tenant appear on in the closing statement?

A) Debit to the seller
B) Credit to the seller
C) Neither A nor B
D) Both A & B

14

A landlord places a term in a lease prohibiting pets on the premises.

Which of the following types of property is illustrated?

A) Control
B) Possession
C) Title
D) Transfer

15

Which of the following describes the practice of a broker depositing trust funds into the firm's operating account?

A) Commingling
B) Diversion
C) Misappropriating
D) Mingling

16

An **agency** is a business or insitution built to provide different or specific services which typically involves organizing transactions between two parties.

Which of the following can be represented by an agent in a single agency?

A) Buyer
B) Seller
C) Either the seller or the buyer
D) Both the seller and the buyer

17

A **circuit breaker** automatically interrupts the flow of electric current when the current goes beyond a preset limit.

Which of the following is the use of a circuit breaker?

A) It distributes the electricity throughout a structure.
B) It muffles the braying of visiting in-laws.
C) It removes the moisture from wiring around bathroom areas.
D) It prevents water from leaking into an attic from the chimney opening.

18

An option to renew is binding for which of the following?

A) Landlord
B) Tenant
C) Both A and B
D) Neither A nor B

19

Which of the following refers to the combining of two or more parcels of land into one tract that has higher total value than the sum of individual plots?

A) Affirmative easement
B) Plottage
C) Plot planting
D) Undue influence

20

Which of the following refers to the only use of lead plumbing pipes?

A) Conduits for electrical lines
B) In the hot water tanks
C) For the incoming water lines
D) None of the above

21

Which of the following will a real estate agent be guilty of if he suggests to a client that it will be better for him to move into an area where he will "fit in"?

A) Steering
B) Redlining
C) Flipping
D) Blockbusting

22

Mutual assent refers to an agreement between two parties to form a contract. It signifies that the parties agree to the terms they are setting, as long as the requirements are in place.

Which of the following refers to mutual assent?

A) Counteroffer
B) Fiduciary offer
C) Lawful objective
D) Meeting of the minds

23

Which of the following refers to a tenant who defaults on a lease but remains in the premises?

A) Codicil
B) Ingrate
C) Tenant at sufferance
D) Tenant by the entirety

24

Fiduciary duties of a real estate agent refer to the broker or agent functions under specific legally mandated duties for a seller or buyer client interests or transactions.

Which of the following categories is under Fiduciary Duties of a Real Estate Agent?

A) Accounting
B) Confidentiality
C) Obedience
D) All of the above

25

Which of the following expenses are not included in calculating net operating income of a rental property?

A) Utility Fees
B) Property taxes
C) Mortgage interest
D) Insurance

26

The **HUD-1 Settlement Statement** was to itemize fees and services charged to the borrower by the broker or lender to apply for a loan for purchasing or refinancing real estate. HUD refers to the Department of Housing and Urban Development.

How long must the parties to a real estate closing be given on reviewing the HUD statement?

A) 3 hours
B) 12 hours
C) 24 hours
D) Three days

27

Which of the following refers to the act of giving a property to a municipal government for public use?

A) Regurgitation
B) Dedication
C) Gestation
D) Grantation

28

A **covenant**, in real property law, is used for conditions tied to the use of land.

Which of the following enforce a covenant in a deed?

A) Court order
B) Habendum clause
C) Local police
D) The condo association

29

The **mortgage's principal and interest payment** is the main component of a monthly mortgage payment. The principal is the amount borrowed and had to be paid back, and interest is what the lender charges for lending money.

Which of the following do mortgage interest and principal payments constitute?

A) Cash flow
B) Debt service
C) Vacancy factor
D) Variable expenses

30

A **Planning and Zoning Commission** refers to locally elected or appointed government board charged with recommending to the local town or city council the boundaries of the various original zoning district and appropriate regulations to be enforced.

To dispute a decision of the planning board, which of the following should a citizen go to?

A) Architectural review board
B) Building inspector
C) Ombudsman
D) Zoning board of appeals

31

Capital expense refers to the money a company spends to buy, maintain, or improve its fixed assets, such as buildings, vehicles, equipment, or land.

Which of the following describes an example of a capital expense that should be considered in property valuation?

A) Fixed rate mortgage payment
B) Property taxes
C) Roof replacement allowance
D) Vacancy

CONTINUE ▶

32

A **rate of return** refers to the loss or gain on an investment over a specified period in the percentage of the investment's cost.

Which of the following is the rate of return of a building earning $80,000 annually that had a purchase price of $750,000?

A) 9.4%
B) 12%
C) 15%
D) 10.6%

33

Which of the following is the organization that develops a set of international building code standards adopted by many states and local governments in the United States?

A) The IMF
B) The World Bank
C) The ICC
D) The UN

34

A **certificate of occupancy** refers to a document issued by a local government agency to certify a building's compliance with applicable building codes and other laws. It indicates that the building is in a condition suitable for occupancy.

When can a Certificate of Occupancy can be issued?

A) After the tax assessor determines the value of the home improvement
B) After a construction job passes the final inspection of the building inspector
C) After a home improvement application is submitted to the building inspector
D) Only after approved plans are submitted

35

Your neighbor has started to raise pigs in his suburban yard which in turn, is stinking up your yard. There are no restrictive covenants or equitable servitudes that apply.

Which of the following is your best way to make the neighbor stop if he won't do so voluntarily utilizing a private method?

A) Filing a private nuisance lawsuit
B) Obtaining an easement
C) Having the city condemn the property
D) There's no private solution available

36

An **exclusive right to sell agreement** is a type of agreement that restricts the seller to list the property with any other agent in which the agent must be paid commission in certain circumstances.

In which of the following scenarios commission does not have to be paid?

A) When the property is not sold
B) When the property is sold by the seller
C) When the property is sold by a cooperating broker
D) When the property is sold by an uncooperative broker

37

Which of the following is the gross income multiplier of a house that rents for $1,400 each month and would sell for $175,000?

A) 120
B) 125
C) 130
D) 300

38

Which of the following is the annual taxes on a property with an assessed value of $750,000 and a tax rate of $2.20 per thousand dollars of assessed value?

A) $1,050
B) $1,650
C) $16,500
D) $10,500

39

A 5-acre parcel of land was sold for $1,750,000. What was the price per square foot? (1 acre = 43,560 square feet)

A) $8.035
B) $40.175
C) $80.350
D) $35,000

40

Economic obsolescence refers to a form of depreciation due to unfavorable external conditions to the property such as the local economy, encroachment of objectionable enterprises, and other factors.

Which of the following describes an example of economic obsolescence?

A) An outmoded air conditioning system
B) A junkyard down the block
C) A dilapidated roof
D) None of the above

41

Multifamily residential refers to multiple separate housing units for residential inhabitants contained in one building or several buildings within one complex.

Which of the following appraisal approaches would appraise multifamily apartment building?

A) Income approach
B) Market data
C) Cost
D) All of the above

42

The **Condominium Act** (Rights of the Unit Owners) requires the unit owners association, as well as its Board of Directors, to comply with the act, and with the condominium's declaration, bylaws, rules and regulations. This act requires that the bylaws specify the methods of selecting and removing board members and the board's powers and duties, including terms of office.

Which of the following about the bylaws of a condominium development is true?

A) They are the regulations by which the Association manages the development
B) It is only a formality to get municipal approvals for the development
C) It is not given to purchasers until binding contracts are signed
D) None of the above

43

Encroachment is where a property owner violates the property rights of his neighbor such as building something on the neighbor's land or allowing something to hang over onto the neighbor's property.

Which of the following could be the least advisable path to take regarding the encroachment on your property?

A) Do nothing.
B) Sue for trespass.
C) Give an easement for encroachment.
D) Sell the property where the encroachment sits to the owner of the encroachment.

44

A **stand-alone house**, also called a single-detached residence, is a free-standing residential building. It is sometimes referred to as a single family home as opposed to a multi-family residential dwelling.

Which of the following is the appraisal approach commonly used in appraising single-family housing?

A) Sales comparison approach
B) Rental approach
C) Income approach
D) Cost approach

45

A home with a market value of $420,000 has insurance for 80% of its market value. If the cost of insurance is $2.05 per $1,000 of insured value, what is the yearly cost of insurance for this home?

A) $688.8
B) $840.0
C) $861.0
D) $1,050

46

PITI refers to a mortgage payment which is the sum of monthly principal, interest, taxes, and insurance.

Which of the following maximum monthly PITI payments would qualify a borrower having a weekly income of $2,200 under the 28% housing ratio guideline?

A) $2,352
B) $2,464
C) $616
D) $1,584

47

An investor requires a 15.5% rate of return. A listed property priced at $1,550,000 has a monthly income of $74,560 and monthly expenses of $54,980.

Does the property meet the investor's requirement? If not, what should the offering price be to meet the demand?

A) Yes.
B) No. $1,478,765.30
C) No. $1,515,870.97
D) No. $1,483,671.15

CONTINUE ▶

A property initially purchased for $1,000,000 increased in value by 7% per year for three years.

Which of the following was the value of the property after the third year?

A) $1,225,043
B) $1,210,000
C) $1,200,000
D) $1,230,000

SECTION 2

#	Answer	Topic	Subtopic	#	Answer	Topic	Subtopic	#	Answer	Topic	Subtopic	#	Answer	Topic	Subtopic
1	D	TA	SA1	13	A	TD	SD2	25	C	TD	SD6	37	B	TA	SA3
2	A	TD	SD4	14	A	TD	SD7	26	C	TD	SD5	38	B	TD	SD6
3	A	TD	SD4	15	A	TB	SB5	27	B	TD	SD2	39	A	TA	SA6
4	B	TB	SB2	16	B	TB	SB4	28	A	TB	SB3	40	B	TD	SD3
5	C	TA	SA7	17	A	TD	SD1	29	B	TA	SA5	41	A	TD	SD6
6	A	TA	SA7	18	A	TD	SD5	30	D	TB	SB6	42	A	TB	SB1
7	A	TA	SA1	19	B	TD	SD4	31	C	TA	SA3	43	A	TD	SD7
8	C	TB	SB3	20	D	TD	SD1	32	D	TA	SA1	44	A	TA	SA3
9	B	TA	SA7	21	A	TD	SD4	33	C	TB	SB3	45	A	TA	SA6
10	D	TD	SD4	22	D	TD	SD5	34	B	TB	SB6	46	B	TA	SA5
11	A	TA	SA2	23	C	TD	SD5	35	A	TB	SB3	47	C	TA	SA5
12	D	TB	SB3	24	D	TB	SB5	36	A	TB	SB4	48	A	TA	SA1

Topics & Subtopics

Code	Description	Code	Description
SA1	Commercial Investment	SB6	Municipal Agencies
SA2	Estates & Interests	SD1	Construction & Environmental Issues
SA3	Income Approach to Real Estate Valuation	SD2	Deeds & Title Closing Costs
SA5	Real Estate Finance	SD3	Property Management
SA6	Real Estate Math	SD4	Real Estate Investment & Analysis
SA7	Real Estate Market	SD5	The contract of sales and leases
SB1	Condominiums & Suites	SD6	Valuation
SB2	Human Rights & Fair Housing	SD7	Forms of Property Ownership
SB3	Land Use & Regulations	TA	Economics
SB4	Law of Agency	TB	Rules & Regulations
SB5	License Law	TD	Transactions & Processes

TEST DIRECTION

DIRECTIONS

Read the questions carefully and then choose the ONE best answer to each question.

Be sure to allocate your time carefully so you are able to complete the entire test within the testing session. You may go back and review your answers at any time.

You may use any available space in your test booklet for scratch work.

Questions in this booklet are not actual test questions but they are the samples for commonly asked questions.

This test aims to cover all topics which may appear on the actual test. However some topics may not be covered.

Studying this booklet will be preparing you for the actual test. It will not guarantee improving your test score but it will help you pass your exam on the first attempt.

Some useful tips for answering multiple choice questions;

- Start with the questions that you can easily answer.

- Underline the keywords in the question.

- Be sure to read all the choices given.

- Watch for keywords such as NOT, always, only, all, never, completely.

- Do not forget to answer every question.

1

Which of the following is issued by a local government indicating that a building is fit for human occupation?

A) Building code
B) Occupancy permit
C) Title
D) Warranty of habitability

2

Which type of consideration does a lot with a fantastic view of the ocean have?

A) Economic
B) Government
C) Physical
D) Social

3

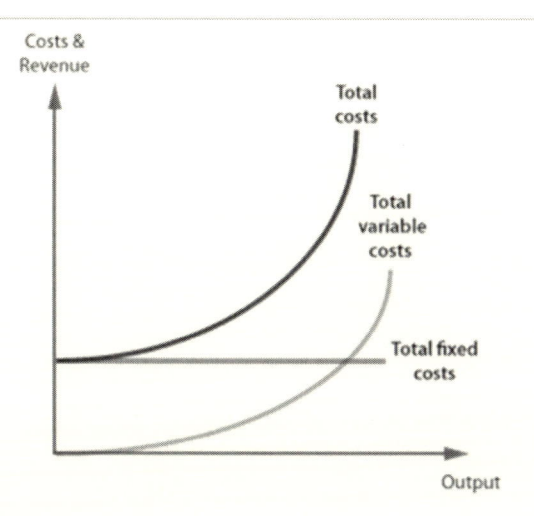

Costs & Revenue graph showing Total costs, Total variable costs, and Total fixed costs vs Output.

Variable cost refers to an expense that varies with production output. Variable costs are those costs that vary depending on volume; they rise as production increases and fall as production decreases. Variable costs differ from fixed costs.

Which of the following is most likely a variable expense?

A) Taxes
B) Heating fuel
C) License fees
D) None of the above

4

An **assessed value** refers to the value assigned to a property to measure applicable taxes.

Which of the following determines the assessed value of a property?

A) Tax Assessor
B) Tax Collector
C) Planning board
D) Municipal council

5

A **printed circuit board** (PCB) is to support and connect electronic parts using conductive pads, tracks and other properties etched from copper sheets laminated onto a non-conductive substrate.

Which of the following have PCBs?

A) Aerosol cans
B) Heating Units
C) Air Condition Systems
D) Electrical equipment

6

Which of the following refers to the document that creates a relationship between a property owner and a broker?

A) State Property Manager License
B) Management Agreement
C) Operating Statement
D) Rent roll

7

Which of the following describes a non-conforming use?

A) It is not legal
B) If the owner changes, it must be removed or closed
C) It does not confirm to the current local zoning laws, but it is permitted because it was existing before
D) None of the above

8

Which of the following organizations establishes a National Register of Historic Places?

A) CERCLA
B) NEPA
C) National Registry Act of 1968
D) National Historical Preservation Act of 1966

9

Which of the following is best defined by market value?

A) The most probable selling price
B) The most recent selling price
C) The listing price
D) Appraised value for property tax purposes

10

Express Agreement is a contract which contains the intentions of the involved parties.

Which of the following is true about an expressed agreement?

A) It can be oral
B) It can be written
C) It is binding on both parties
D) All of the above

11

A landlord has the right to deny a tenant to rent his dwelling due to certain circumstances which the State Laws allow.

Which of the following will the State Laws allow a landlord to refuse to rent to a tenant?

A) Rock musician
B) People with dogs
C) Prison records
D) All of the above

12

Which of the following document is issued when an improvement is made to a property and the building inspector passes it?

A) Deed
B) Tax assessment
C) Building permit
D) Certificate of Occupancy

13

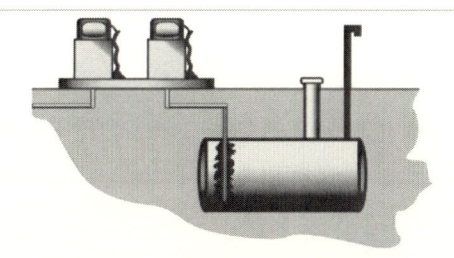

Which of the following describes the primary risk to the environment from underground storage tanks?

A) Toxic materials can leak from the ruptured tanks
B) Wildlife can drink from the open ends
C) There can be emission of fumes into the air from faulty vents
D) None of the above

14

A deed is a legal document that is signed and delivered regarding the ownership of property or legal rights.

Which of the following is needed for a deed to be valid?

A) It must be in triplicate
B) It must be signed by the grantor
C) It must be signed by the grantee
D) All of the above

15

Mary has the right to use a path which crosses her neighbor's property to reach a public street.

Which of the following is the best description of her property right?

A) Possession
B) Control
C) Easement
D) Restrictive covenant

16

An **open market** is an unrestricted market with free access and competition of buyers and sellers.

Which of the following refers to the most probable price a property would be sold for in an open market?

A) Appraised value
B) Cost
C) Market Value
D) Seller's value

17

An **agent** is a seller acting upon the authority of an owner while the client is the one that is buying goods or properties through the agent.

Which of the following best describes the act of an agent following lawful instructions of a client?

A) Care
B) Loyalty
C) Obedience
D) Accounting

18

A **commercial lease** is for tenants using the property for commercial purposes such as business versus residential use.

At the end of a commercial lease, which of the following does the trade fixtures belong to?

A) Tenant
B) Landlord
C) Agent
D) None of the above

19

Security means any written, electronic or oral agreement that is secured by any lien or charge upon the capital, assets, profits, property or credit of any person or any public or governmental body, subdivision, or agency.

Which of the following refers to security in a real state?

A) An apartment building owned in a partnership
B) Real Estate Investment Trust shares
C) Both A and B
D) Neither A nor B

20

A **minor** under the law refers to a person under a certain age that is usually the age of majority which is the shift from childhood to adulthood. Generally, depending upon your state law, the age of majority is at some point between **18** and **21**. It also depends on jurisdiction and application.

Which of the following is a contract entered into by a minor?

A) Voidable
B) Void
C) Valid
D) Exculpatory

21

A **Condemnation Suit** is a type of judicial proceeding filed against a property owner.

Which of the following is the condition when a Condemnation Suit is filed against a property owner?

A) Escheat
B) Incentive zoning
C) Eminent Domain
D) Variance

22

Torrens title is a type of land registration which a register of land holdings maintained by the state guarantees an indefeasible title to those included in the register.

Which of the following investigates the title to a parcel of property seeking to be registered in a state that uses the Torrens Title System?

A) A judge
B) A retained attorney
C) The Examiner of Title
D) The Registrar of Title

CONTINUE ▶

23

A **transfer tax** refers to a tax on the passing of property title to another person.

Which of the following usually pays the transfer taxes?

A) Closing Attorney
B) Lender
C) Seller
D) Buyer

24

Which of the following component of the NHPA (National Historic Preservation Act) is concerned with the assessment of a proposed project involving a property listed on the National Register of Historic Places?

A) EAS
B) EIS
C) Section 106 review process
D) None of the answers are correct.

25

A **security deposit** refers to the total amunt of money held in trust which is sometimes for an initial part-payment in a purchasing process.

Which of the following is the reason why the landlord maintains security deposits?

A) To be used to repair damage to the unit above and beyond normal wear and tear
B) To keep tenants from moving out before the lease is up
C) To force a renewal of the lease by the tenant
D) In the event, a fire destroys the building

26

A Mortgage Broker, specializing in real estate transactions, acts as the middleman between a client (a person or a company) and a specific bank.

The client's financial ability to pay a potential mortagage is reviewed to decide if the client is financially established for the bank to back their real estate purchase.

Which of the following mostly involves a mortgage broker?

A) Originating loan applications
B) Providing the mortgage loan funds
C) Property value determination
D) All of the above

27

A **rate of return** refers to the loss or gain on an investment over a specified period of time in the percentage of the investment's cost.

An investment property's monthly net income is $18,240, and its monthly operating expenses are $11,120. If the investor paid $824,500 for the property, which of the following is the investor's rate of return?

A) 1.2%
B) 8.6%
C) 10.36%
D) 14.8%

28

Collateral is a property or asset that a borrower offers as a way for a lender to secure the loan.

Which of the following collaterals is needed for a co-op purchaser to purchase a loan?

A) A co-op building stock
B) A bond
C) A property deed
D) Title policy

29

When Aries bought his property he had a 20% down payment and secured a 30 year loan at 6.5% interest.

Which of the following was the price of the property if his first month's payment was $1,137.72?

A) $180,000
B) $135,000
C) $225,000
D) $410,000

30

Which of the following will happen to an apartment under a lease that becomes unusable due to smoke from a fire in an adjacent unit?

A) It is the landlord's responsibility to immediately terminate the lease
B) The requirement of the tenant to remain in the apartment until it is condemned
C) It is termed an actual eviction
D) It is termed a constructive eviction

31

Alexandria's house is the eldest home in her neighborhood. However, her property has been valued higher than she expected.

Which of the following principles of valuation is likely at play?

A) Principle of progression
B) Principle of contribution
C) Principle of regression
D) Principle of highest and best use

32

A parcel of property having an area of 2,760,000 square feet has a width of 2,400 feet.

How deep is the property?

A) 780 feet
B) 900 feet
C) 1,150 feet
D) 3,200 feet

33

Interested house buyer can often approach a lender, and the lender can provide assurances he would be able to get a loan up to a certain amount.

Which of the following is involved in a pre-approval letter?

A) An application that is made under oath
B) Affidavit of an underwriter
C) Bonding of the borrowers
D) Verification of employment and credit history

34

A lot that measures 840 foot in length and 670 foot in width was sold for $2,532,600.

Which of the following was the cost per square foot?

A) $2.50
B) $2.75
C) $4.25
D) $4.50

35

Which of the following is the definition of adverse possession?

A) Giving up property voluntarily to the government
B) A legal proceeding to divide property owned by two or more people
C) The sudden loss of land by an act of nature like a landslide
D) A person who does not have legal title acquires legal ownership based on occupation of the land without the permission of its legal owner

36

Which of the following refers to a public restriction on how a person can use his/her land situated in a particular area of town?

A) Easement
B) Profit a pendre
C) Restrictive covenant
D) Zoning ordinance

37

In the United States, a **historic district** is a group of buildings, properties, or sites that have been designated by one of several entities on different levels as historically or architecturally significant.

Which of the following areas of a historic district requires permission to alter?

A) Dining areas
B) Plumbing fixtures
C) The interior of a building
D) The exterior of a building

38

A mortgage broker is a middleman that is working with a borrower and a lender while qualifying the borrower for a mortgage.

The broker gathers income, asset and employment documentations, a credit report and other information for assessing the borrower's ability to secure financing.

Which of the following can compensate a mortgage broker?

A) The lender
B) The borrower
C) Neither A nor B
D) Both A and B

39

Front foot is a standard measurement of land, applied at the frontage of its street line. It is used for lots of generally uniform depth in downtown areas.

A property with dimensions of 125 foot frontage and 250 foot depth was sold for $1,750,000. What was the price of the property per front foot?

A) $70.00
B) $1,400.00
C) $8,750.00
D) $14,000.00

40

National Environmental Policy Act (NEPA) is an environmental law imposed in the United States to promote the enhancement of the environment and established the President's Council on Environmental Quality (CEQ).

Which of the following refers to a report issued under NEPA on a proposed project?

A) Environmental Impact Statement
B) Environmental Assessment Statement
C) Section 106 report
D) None of the answers are correct.

41

A **Real Estate License** is the authorization issued by state government, giving agents and brokers the ability to legally represent a home seller or buyer in the process of buying or selling real estate.

Which of the following individual is required to have a real estate license according to State Real Estate Laws?

A) Auctioneer
B) Executor
C) Practicing Attorney
D) None of the above

42

Shiem is looking to buy a property that costs $115,000. The property can be rented for $750 per month. She has done her research and determined the net operating expenses to be $4,000 per year. Her desired cap rate is 6%.

Which of the following is the appraisal value of this property, rounded to the nearest dollar, using the income capitalization approach?

A) $34,000
B) $66,666
C) $83,333
D) $106,950

43

Zeus imparts a part of his real property to Chris so long as the property is for residential purposes; if it ceases to be used for residential purposes, Brent will receive the property in fee simple.

What type of future interest does Brent have?

A) A contingent remainder
B) A vested remainder
C) A reversion
D) An executory interest

44

Conservative investing is a type of investment strategy that seeks to preserve an investment portfolio's value by investing in lower risk securities. Conservative investors have their risk tolerance range from low to moderate. Some good examples of conservative investing strategies are capital preservation and current income.

Which of the following should a conservative investor consider in order to conserve the capital?

A) Regional shopping malls
B) Industrial parks
C) Highly leveraged properties
D) Fee simple purchases

45

Which of the following may compensate a residential apartment building manager?

A) Key money
B) Rebates from fuel oil suppliers
C) Percentage of collected rents
D) Kickbacks from maintenance service companies

46

Earnest money refers to a deposit made to a seller showing the buyer's good faith in a transaction.

Which of the following does an earnest money deposit appear on a closing statement?

A) Debit to seller
B) Debit to buyer
C) Credit to seller
D) Credit to buyer

47

Kristine has offered to purchase Clyde's house which has pending results of a property inspection. The report indicates that the roof needs to be repaired. Kristine asks Clyde to fix the roof.

Which of the following is not a viable option for Clyde?

A) Offer a lower purchase price.
B) Refuse to make the repairs.
C) Refuse and keep the earnest money.
D) Repair the roof.

48

A salesperson sold a property for $312,000. The salesperson's commission was 20% of the 6% commission paid by the owner.

After buying a gift for the new homeowners valued at $120, the salesperson will take home how much money?

A) $3,624
B) $3,744
C) $3,864
D) $3,920

SECTION 3

#	Answer	Topic	Subtopic	#	Answer	Topic	Subtopic	#	Answer	Topic	Subtopic	#	Answer	Topic	Subtopic
1	B	TB	SB3	13	A	TD	SD1	25	A	TD	SD5	37	D	TB	SB6
2	C	TA	SA1	14	B	TD	SD2	26	A	TA	SA5	38	D	TA	SA4
3	B	TD	SD3	15	C	TD	SD7	27	C	TA	SA3	39	D	TA	SA1
4	A	TB	SB3	16	C	TD	SD3	28	A	TB	SB1	40	A	TB	SB3
5	D	TD	SD1	17	C	TB	SB4	29	C	TA	SA4	41	A	TB	SB5
6	B	TD	SD3	18	A	TD	SD5	30	D	TD	SD5	42	C	TA	SA3
7	C	TB	SB3	19	B	TD	SD4	31	A	TA	SA7	43	B	TD	SD7
8	D	TB	SB3	20	A	TD	SD5	32	C	TA	SA6	44	B	TA	SA1
9	A	TA	SA7	21	C	TB	SB3	33	D	TA	SA6	45	C	TD	SD3
10	D	TB	SB4	22	C	TD	SD7	34	D	TA	SA2	46	D	TD	SD2
11	D	TB	SB2	23	C	TD	SD2	35	D	TB	SB6	47	C	TA	SA7
12	D	TB	SB3	24	C	TB	SB3	36	D	TA	SA7	48	A	TA	SA6

Topics & Subtopics

Code	Description	Code	Description
SA1	Commercial Investment	SB5	License Law
SA2	Estates & Interests	SB6	Municipal Agencies
SA3	Income Approach to Real Estate Valuation	SD1	Construction & Environmental Issues
SA4	Mortgage Brokerage	SD2	Deeds & Title Closing Costs
SA5	Real Estate Finance	SD3	Property Management
SA6	Real Estate Math	SD4	Real Estate Investment & Analysis
SA7	Real Estate Market	SD5	The contract of sales and leases
SB1	Condominiums & Suites	SD7	Forms of Property Ownership
SB2	Human Rights & Fair Housing	TA	Economics
SB3	Land Use & Regulations	TB	Rules & Regulations
SB4	Law of Agency	TD	Transactions & Processes

TEST DIRECTION

DIRECTIONS

Read the questions carefully and then choose the ONE best answer to each question.

Be sure to allocate your time carefully so you are able to complete the entire test within the testing session. You may go back and review your answers at any time.

You may use any available space in your test booklet for scratch work.

Questions in this booklet are not actual test questions but they are the samples for commonly asked questions.

This test aims to cover all topics which may appear on the actual test. However some topics may not be covered.

Studying this booklet will be preparing you for the actual test. It will not guarantee improving your test score but it will help you pass your exam on the first attempt.

Some useful tips for answering multiple choice questions;

- Start with the questions that you can easily answer.

- Underline the keywords in the question.

- Be sure to read all the choices given.

- Watch for keywords such as NOT, always, only, all, never, completely.

- Do not forget to answer every question.

1

Net operating income is a calculation used in analyzing real estate investments that generate income.

Which of the following are some sources of revenue for calculating the net operating income?

A) Parking fees
B) Rent payments
C) Vending machine profits
D) All of these are correct answers

2

Which of the following describes the part of a lease that states the intention of the lessor and the lessee?

A) Allowance clause
B) Demising clause
C) Usage clause
D) Passage clause

3

The government has the right to arrest and imprison any suspicious individual on the basis of rightful State Laws.

Which of the following does this situation correspond to?

A) Police Power
B) Escheat
C) Eminent Domain
D) None of the above

4

Which of the following state laws protect investors from a lack of vetted information?

A) Blank Slate Laws
B) Blue Sky Laws
C) The Securities Act of 1933
D) None of these answers are correct.

5

Which of the following does a purchaser need to produce at the closing?

A) One year homeowner insurance policy
B) Deed to the property
C) Tenant lease
D) Certificate of Occupancy

6

Which of the following is granted by a deed wherein the property may revert to the grantor of the deed if the condition is not to be met by the grantee of the deed?

A) Indefeasible fee
B) Defeasible fee
C) Fee simple
D) None of the answers are correct.

CONTINUE ▶

7

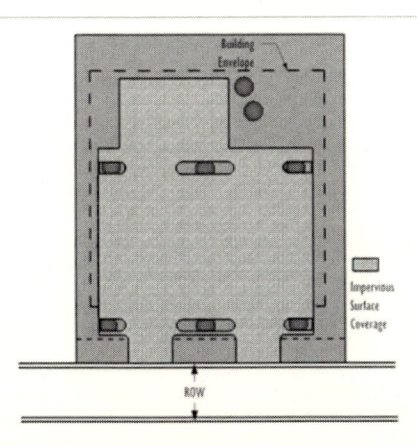

Setbacks refer to the imposed building restrictions on property owners. Local governments create setbacks through ordinances and Building Codes according to public policies such as safety, privacy, and environmental protection.

Which of the following refers to the setback?

A) Judgment
B) Sheathing
C) Disappointment
D) Mandated distance

8

A **property inspection** is an inspection of a building by professionally trained and experienced people. During the inspection, buildings and their components are evaluated.

During a professional property inspection, which of the following is inspected?

A) Foundation
B) Heating
C) Land
D) All of these are inspected.

9

Site analysis refers to a preliminary phase of architectural and urban design processes dedicated to the study of the climatic, geographical, historical, legal, and infrastructural context of a specific site.

Which of the following does not belong to the physical factors considered in performing a site analysis?

A) Location
B) Shape
C) Size
D) Zoning

10

An **elected official** refers to a person who is an official by an election. Which of the following are not elected?

A) City Council members
B) Board of Trustee members
C) Planning Board members
D) Town Council members

11

Dual agency is a situation in which real estate agent works with both the buyer and the seller.

Which of the following scenario best describes Dual Agency?

A) A real estate broker operating two real estate offices
B) It is illegal if both parties don't have knowledge and consent
C) A combination of real estate and insurance being offered at the same time
D) A method whereby two sales agents split a commission on a transaction

12

Which of the following is the massive wooden members that sit atop the foundation wall and upon which the frame is placed?

A) Girders
B) Joists
C) Bridging
D) Sills

13

Property valuation refers to the process of creating an opinion of value for real property.

Which of the following is not one of the four foundational elements of property valuation?

A) Demand
B) Supply
C) Transferability
D) Scarcity

14

Lead refers to a naturally occurring element which is found in small amounts in the crust of earth.

Which of the following must the EPA booklet entitled "Protect Your Family from Lead in Your Home" be given to?

A) Everyone
B) Brokers
C) Sellers
D) Purchasers

15

A **septic tank** is a chamber usually underground where domestic wastewater flows for basic treatment.

Which of the following agencies sets the requirements for well and septic systems?

A) Department of Taxation
B) State Department of Environmental Conservation
C) Department of Health
D) Environmental Protection Agency

16

The **binding contract** refers to an agreement in writing between two or more individuals. If one negates to his/her promise as outlined in the contract, a court can impose penalties in the event.

Which of the following must be given to a person before signing a binding contract to purchase a condominium?

A) A bond
B) A blank contract
C) A survey
D) A Public Offering Statement

17

Which of the following is a contract that binds only one party?

A) Binder
B) Unilateral contract
C) Bilateral contract
D) Implied contract

18

Which of the following must a licensee do when she is selling her property?

A) Disclose the fact she is a licensed real estate agent to prospective buyers
B) List the property at a fair market value
C) List the property with the MLS
D) All of the above

19

A **feasibility study** refers to an analysis of the success of a project's completion, accounting for factors like economic, technological, legal and scheduling. Project managers use feasibility studies to study the positive and negative outcomes of a project before investing.

Which of the following does a feasibility study in Real Estate determine?

A) Whether to undertake an investment or not
B) The location for a successful investment
C) The value of an investment
D) None of the above

20

A **joint tenancy** is an ownership wherein each co-tenant owns an undivided share of the property just as in a tenancy in common. Four conditions are required for the formation of joint tenancy. Three of them are time, title and possession.

Which of the following is the fourth condition?

A) Incontinence
B) Interest
C) Loyalty
D) Trust

21

A **community** describes a group of people living in the same place or having a particular characteristic in common.

Which of the following should a board create to develop a community?

A) Architectural review board
B) Board of trustees
C) Building department
D) Master plan

22

Property management refers to the control, oversight, and operation of a real estate. Management describes the need to be cared for, monitored and accounted for its useful life and condition.

Which of the following documents does a real estate broker prepare to obtain a property management job?

A) Deed analysis
B) Property survey
C) Financial statement
D) Management proposal

23

Licensee refers to a person or business that holds an approved license to conduct an activity, such as operating a business.

With which of the following can a licensee share an earned commission?

A) Seller
B) Customer
C) No one
D) Postal worker providing a lead

24

John is working as a municipal tax assessor. Which of the following is John's role?

A) He sets the tax collector's goals
B) He determines the value of properties in the community
C) He determines the tax rate property owners pay
D) He collects taxes from property owners

25

Ryan presents an offer to purchase Maria's house. He includes a provision which states that he can terminate the contract if an inspection reveals that necessary repairs to the house will exceed one percent of the purchase price.

Which of the following is the best description of this clause?

A) A cost of repair clause
B) An escape clause
C) An inspection clause
D) None of the answers are correct.

26

A **life estate** refers to the land ownership for a person's lifetime in common and statutory law.

For which of the following can life estate be created?

A) Only a relative
B) Any person
C) Only a trustee
D) None of the above

27

Tax deduction refers to a reduction of income which is taxed and commonly a result of expenses from those incurred to produce additional income.

For which of the following can a homeowner take an income tax deduction?

A) Real estate taxes
B) Paid mortgage interest
C) Paid student loan interest
D) All of the above

28

A **first mortgage** refers to a mortgage in a first lien position on the property that secures the mortgage. A first mortgage has priority over all other liens or claims on a property in the event of default.

Which of the following are the highest priority liens?

A) Tax liens
B) Commercial liens
C) Mortgage liens
D) None of the above

29

A **property tax** or also called **millage rate** is a tax on the value of a property levied by the governing authority of the jurisdiction in the location of the property.

Which of the following impacts does depreciation have on real estate taxation?

A) Depreciation adds up to the basis and is only essential for taxes when the property is sold.
B) Depreciation refers to the total of all maintenance expenses associated with an aging house.
C) Depreciation lets the owner in taking a paper loss against the income of the property.
D) Depreciation lowers land value for local property taxes.

30

Which of the following is required to qualify as a limited partnership?

A) At least one general partner and one limited partner
B) Two or more limited partners and an annual franchise fee paid to the state
C) At least two general partners and registration with the state
D) At least two general partners

31

The **income approach** refers to a real estate appraisal method that allows investors to estimate the value of a property by taking the net operating income of the rent collected and dividing it by the capitalization rate.

Which of the following is a method in the income approach to property valuation?

A) Direct capitalization
B) Discounted cash flow
C) Gross income multiplier
D) All of these are correct

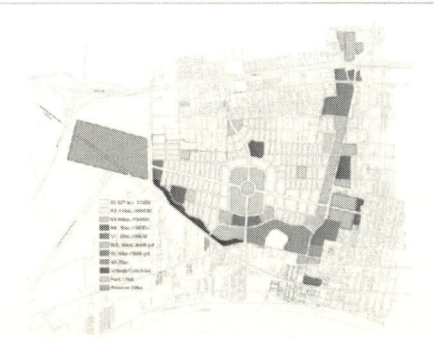

32

Zoning is a legal mechanism for local governments to regulate the use of privately owned real properties. Through community planning and development, zoning laws help local governmental agencies preserve property values and ensure that communities are functional and safe places.

Which of the following is not affected by Zoning?

A) Private property
B) The interior of a building
C) The number of parking spaces for a fast food restaurant
D) The distance a structure may be erected from a property line

33

A **mechanic's lien** refers to the security interest in property's title for the benefit of those who have supplied materials or labor that gives improvement to the property.

Which of the following places a mechanics lien on a property?

A) Administrator
B) Former owner
C) Home improvement contractor
D) Owner

34

Cooperative housing is another type of home ownership. Instead of owning an actual real estate with cooperative housing, you own a part of a corporation that owns the building. Cooperative housing usually includes an apartment building or buildings.

Which type of income is not considered in a loan application for a cooperative unit purchase?

A) Barter income
B) Gambling
C) Commissions
D) Alimony

35

Which of the following ownership form exists when a corporation owns real estate?

A) By the entirety
B) In trust
C) Tenants in common
D) In severalty

36

A **real estate investment trust** (REIT) means that a company operates or finances income-producing real estate.

Which of the following describes the process of taxing REIT dividends?

A) REIT dividends tax at corporate income tax rates.
B) Dividends tax at capital gains rates.
C) Investors will pay taxes on dividends at the maximum federal income tax rate.
D) Investors pay taxes on dividends at their income tax rate.

37

When Fred bought his property he had a 20% down payment and secured a 30 year loan at 7% interest.

Which of the following is the amount he paid for the property if his first month's payment was $2,240.00?

A) $260,000
B) $290,000
C) $422,000
D) $480,000

38

Which of the following refers to the general term in real estate that means a person legally owns a piece of real estate and has the right to use and enjoy it?

A) Equitable title
B) Legal title
C) Title
D) All of the answers are correct.

39

A **landlord** is an individual who rents a land, a building, or an apartment to a tenant.

Which of the following should not be the basis where the landlord refuses a tenant?

A) Number of children in the family
B) Prison record of the tenants
C) Political affiliation of the tenants
D) All of the above

40

A rental property brings in a $750 monthly rent and has annual net operating expenses of $5,500.

Which of the following is the net operating income of this property?

A) $2,000
B) $4,750
C) $3,500
D) $14,500

CONTINUE ▶

41

David and Erika live in a state which recognizes dower and courtesy and also has enacted a statute entitling a surviving spouse an elective share of the deceased spouse's estate. Dave decides to disinherit Erika.

Which of the following is correct?

A) Erika loses her dower interest because David disinherited her.
B) Erika may elect the rightful share or claim her dower interest.
C) Erika loses her right to an elective share because she has been disinherited by will.
D) None of the answers are correct.

42

You referred a client to a lender. In return they sent you a thank you note with a $100 gift card to a local restaurant.

Which of the following law makes this kickback illegal?

A) CRA
B) ECOA
C) RESPA
D) Regulation Z

43

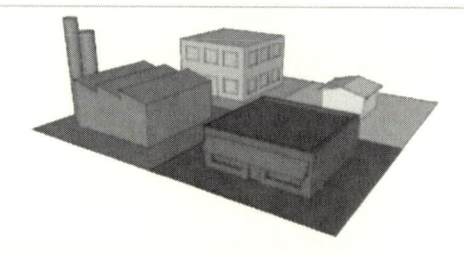

Zoning refers to the division of land in a municipality into zones in which specific land uses are permitted or prohibited.

Which of the following types of zoning would be most appropriate for a mall or a group of stores?

A) Agriculture
B) Commercial
C) Residential
D) Rural

44

Which of the following follows the correct formula for rate of return?

A) (Investment Gain - Investment Cost) / Investment Cost
B) Investment Gain / Investment Cost
C) (Investment Gain + Investment Cost) / Investment Cost
D) (Investment Gain - Investment Cost) / Investment Gain

CONTINUE ▶

45

An **independent contractor** is an individual, business, or corporation that provides goods or services to another entity under terms specified in a contract.

In which of the following scenarios will the Federal Government accept a sales agent as an independent contractor?

A) The agent earns no money
B) The agent has another job
C) The agent works out of his or her own home
D) The agent is paid strictly on a commission basis

46

What type of loans are not insured or guaranteed by the US Government?

A) Conventional loans
B) FHA loans
C) VA loans
D) All of the above

47

Federal Agencies are special government organizations which have been set up for specific purposes such as the management of different resources, financial oversight of industries or national security issues.

Which of the following is the federal agency concerned with environmental matters?

A) DEC
B) EPA
C) FHA
D) SOB

A **cash flow statement** refers to the financial statement showing the changes in balance sheet accounts and how income affects cash and cash equivalents, and breaks the analysis down to operating, investing and financing activities.

Which of the following is the correct formula for the total cash flow statement?

A) Rental Cash Statement + Investing Cash Statement + Financing Cash Statement

B) Operations Cash Statement + Investing Cash Statement + Financing Cash Statement

C) Operations Cash Statement + Purchase Cash Statement + Sale Cash Statement

D) Operations Cash Statement + Tax Cash Statement + Financing Cash Statement

SECTION 4

#	Answer	Topic	Subtopic	#	Answer	Topic	Subtopic	#	Answer	Topic	Subtopic	#	Answer	Topic	Subtopic
1	D	TA	SA3	13	B	TA	SA2	25	A	TA	SA7	37	C	TA	SA2
2	B	TD	SD5	14	D	TD	SD1	26	B	TA	SA2	38	C	TD	SD7
3	D	TB	SB3	15	C	TD	SD1	27	D	TA	SA5	39	C	TB	SB2
4	B	TD	SD4	16	D	TB	SB1	28	A	TA	SA2	40	C	TA	SA3
5	A	TD	SD2	17	B	TD	SD5	29	C	TD	SD4	41	B	TD	SD7
6	B	TB	SB3	18	A	TB	SB5	30	A	TD	SD4	42	C	TB	SB5
7	D	TB	SB3	19	A	TA	SA1	31	D	TA	SA3	43	B	TB	SB3
8	D	TA	SA7	20	B	TA	SA2	32	B	TB	SB3	44	A	TD	SD4
9	D	TA	SA2	21	D	TB	SB6	33	C	TA	SA2	45	D	TB	SB4
10	C	TB	SB2	22	D	TD	SD3	34	B	TB	SB1	46	A	TA	SA5
11	B	TB	SB4	23	C	TB	SB5	35	D	TA	SA1	47	B	TD	SD1
12	D	TD	SD1	24	B	TB	SB6	36	D	TD	SD4	48	B	TD	SD4

Topics & Subtopics

Code	Description	Code	Description
SA1	Commercial Investment	SB6	Municipal Agencies
SA2	Estates & Interests	SD1	Construction & Environmental Issues
SA3	Income Approach to Real Estate Valuation	SD2	Deeds & Title Closing Costs
SA5	Real Estate Finance	SD3	Property Management
SA7	Real Estate Market	SD4	Real Estate Investment & Analysis
SB1	Condominiums & Suites	SD5	The contract of sales and leases
SB2	Human Rights & Fair Housing	SD7	Forms of Property Ownership
SB3	Land Use & Regulations	TA	Economics
SB4	Law of Agency	TB	Rules & Regulations
SB5	License Law	TD	Transactions & Processes

TEST DIRECTION

DIRECTIONS

Read the questions carefully and then choose the ONE best answer to each question.

Be sure to allocate your time carefully so you are able to complete the entire test within the testing session. You may go back and review your answers at any time.

You may use any available space in your test booklet for scratch work.

Questions in this booklet are not actual test questions but they are the samples for commonly asked questions.

This test aims to cover all topics which may appear on the actual test. However some topics may not be covered.

Studying this booklet will be preparing you for the actual test. It will not guarantee improving your test score but it will help you pass your exam on the first attempt.

Some useful tips for answering multiple choice questions;

- Start with the questions that you can easily answer.

- Underline the keywords in the question.

- Be sure to read all the choices given.

- Watch for keywords such as NOT, always, only, all, never, completely.

- Do not forget to answer every question.

1

Which of the following would not refer to a transaction where parents are selling to their son and daughter-in-law?

A) Valid
B) Recordable
C) Enforceable
D) An arm's length transaction

2

A **mortgage broker** functions as a middleman who brokers mortgage loans to others on behalf of individuals or businesses.

Which of the following should mortgage brokers disclose to loan applicants as a requirement?

A) Fees
B) Net worth
C) Amount of credit line
D) All of the above

3

Which of the following choices below is the best description of a condominium (usually known as a condo)?

A) Special form of cooperative ownership
B) Special form of residential and commercial ownership
C) Special form of cooperative and condominium ownership
D) Special form of condominium ownership

4

When determining a property's value and a budget, which of the following expense accounts for the possibility that the property will not have a paying tenant?

A) Capital expense
B) Replacement allowance
C) Tenancy
D) Vacancy

5

Timeshare refers to the arrangement where joint owners have the right to use a property as a vacation home under a time-sharing agreement.

Which of the following types of timeshare does not give you any ownership interest over the property but lets you use the property for a specific period?

A) Licensed timeshare
B) An RTU (Right to Use) contract
C) A fixed term timeshare
D) None of the above

6

Which among the following business structures does not require registration with the state?

A) S Corp
B) General Partnership
C) C Corp
D) LLC

7

Which of the following is required when selling real estate securities?

A) A real estate agent license
B) A Series 7 license
C) Registration with the state
D) All of these answers are correct.

8

Which of the following refers to the outside rough surface of a frame structure placed over the studs?

A) Sheathing
B) Paneling
C) Molding
D) Eaves

9

A **land patent** is an exclusive land grant made by a sovereign entity with respect to a particular tract of land.

Which of the following is the use of a land patent?

A) To convey a public land to an individual
B) To fasten two parallel plates at a corner
C) To fasten two different plates at a corner
D) To correct an irregularity in a zoning law

10

Closing refers to the last step in executing a real estate transaction which is set during the negotiation phase and usually takes several weeks after the offer is formally accepted.

Which of the following is not necessary at a closing?

A) Listing Agent
B) Deed
C) Seller
D) Buyer

11

Which of the following offers the greatest assurance of title?

A) Warranty deed
B) Sheriff's deed
C) Quitclaim deed
D) Bargain and Sale deed

12

When you request a mortgage, lenders look for specific financial characteristics about you to decide whether or not you are in a credit risk.

What is used by financial institutions to determine loan amounts for borrowers?

A) Amortization tables
B) Apportionments
C) Quadrennial factors
D) Qualifying ratios

13

Deed refers to a legal document which is an official record and proof of ownership of property.

Which of the following is a must for deeds to be recorded?

A) Written
B) Acknowledged
C) Both A and B
D) Neither A nor B

14

Mortgage brokers help a client find the best interest rates and terms for a mortgage. Mortagage brokers need to be licensed to work independently and legally.

Which of the following registers mortgage brokers?

A) Department of State
B) Department of Banking
C) Department of Brokerage
D) Department of Mortgage Brokerage

15

How do unused prepaid taxes appear on a closing statement?

A) As a credit to the seller
B) As a credit to the buyer
C) Neither A nor B
D) Both A and B

16

A **gross lease** is a lease where the tenant pays a flat rental amount, and the landlord pays for all property charges regularly incurred by the ownership.

Which of the following is true about a gross lease?

A) It requires the tenant to pay taxes and insurance
B) It only applies to commercial properties.
C) It is vile and repulsive
D) None of the above

17

Market value should exchange on the date of valuation between a willing buyer and a willing seller in an arms-length transaction after proper marketing wherein the parties had each acted knowledgeably and prudently.

Which of the following refers to the factor that exerts the least amount of influence on the value of a seller's property?

A) Local economy
B) The listing agent's opinion
C) Location
D) Supply and demand

18

An **encumbrance** is a kind of regulation, liability, charge, or claim that is legally binding upon a property of an individual or entity. This may affect the clarity of a good title or may diminish the value of the property, but may not prevent transfer of title.

Which of the following can be a form of encumberance?

A) Shared driveway
B) Right of Way
C) Real estate tax lien
D) All of the above

19

If a property is worth $400,000 and an investor expects to be able to earn a net operating income of $22,000 a year, what is the desired cap rate?

A) 22%
B) 11%
C) 6.5%
D) 5.5%

20

Which of the following does the IRS use to define a real estate professional?

A) Whether the taxpayer is a licensed real estate agent or not
B) The number of hours worked in real estate each year
C) The number of real estate properties owned
D) The number of experience years in the real estate industry

CONTINUE ▶

21

Which of the following is the best description of the discounted cash flow method?

A) The sum of the future value of rents over a specified period of time
B) The ratio of the rent over the selling price of the dwelling
C) The sum of the present value of the rents over a specified period of time
D) A discount that is paid upon purchase since the seller guarantees cash flow

22

When someone dies having made a valid will, he or she dies "testate." Otherwise, he or she died "intestate."

A person died "testate," but after an extensive search, there were no additional heirs found.

By which of the following ways should the person's real property be transferred?

A) Devise
B) Demise
C) Escheat to the state
D) Descent and distribution

23

A **life estate** refers to the land ownership for a person's lifetime in common and statutory law. However, in legal terms, it is an estate that will terminate at death in which a property can transfer to another person or revert to the original owner.

Which of the following is the interest in a life estate held by a grantor?

A) Primary interest
B) Interest rate
C) Remainder Interest
D) Reversionary interest

24

Which of the following type of arrangements is useful when companies need to unbind the invested money in an asset for other investments, but the asset still needs to operate?

A) Sale and leaseback
B) Secondary market
C) Joint venture
D) Contingency

CONTINUE ▶

25

Condominiums are classified as real state properties, meaning that buyers own the deeds to their dwellings. Buying into a co-op lets you become a shareholder in the corporation entitled of the property. As a shareholder, you are qualified for the exclusive use of a housing unit in the property.

Which of the following should a prospective co-op purchaser have to meet?

A) The Board of Directors
B) The broker's attorney
C) The building superintendent
D) The city council

26

Installment sale contract refers to the method of sale allowing for partial deferral of capital gain to any future taxation years.

In an installment sale contract on a property, when is the title conveyed to the purchaser?

A) When the last payment has been turned over to the seller
B) When the contract is signed
C) At the end of the rescission period
D) When the full down payment has been turned over to the seller's attorney

CONTINUE ▶

27

A **condominium** is a type of real estate divided into several units that are each separately owned, surrounded by common areas jointly owned.

Which of the following does condominium purchase involve?

A) Deed transfer
B) Meeting with a Board of Directors
C) Purchase of corporate stock
D) Proprietary Lease

28

Which of the following types of scam entails homeowners who are encouraged to refinance their property over and over until little or no equity remains?

A) Reverse equity
B) Property skimming
C) Loan flipping
D) Extreme lending

29

Which of the following power permits the government to take your private property even if you don't want it to do so?

A) Zoning laws
B) Environmental regulations
C) Eminent domain
D) None. Such government action is unconstitutional.

30

Which of the following requires the federal government to consider the environmental impact of its projects?

A) CERCLA
B) NEPA
C) NHPA
D) None of the above

31

Which of the following is true regarding desired profit that an investor uses to determine the value of a property?

A) Increasing expenses reach the desired profit.
B) The desired profit is a personal choice for each investor.
C) The desired profit does not affect property valuation.
D) The desired profit is one percent of the purchase price each month.

32

Which of the following is true for specific performance as a remedy granted by a court?

A) It requires a party to a contract to pay a specific amount of money damages
B) It requires a party to a contract to renegotiate the contract
C) It requires a party to a contract to perform on the contract
D) It voids the contract

33

Which of the following federal laws requires the Good Faith Estimate to be provided by the borrower within three business days after taking a loan application?

A) TILA
B) RESPA
C) HMDA
D) ECOA

34

Zoning laws in Belleville Township requires an apartment building to provide one and a half parking spaces for every 1,000 square feet of inhabited space.

A local apartment building has 60,000 square feet of apartments. How many parking spaces should it have?

A) 200
B) 180
C) 120
D) 90

35

A copper mine was considered as the town's biggest employer which recently closed. House values have collapsed, and houses have become difficult to sell at any price.

What type of consideration is given above?

A) Economic
B) Government
C) Physical
D) Social

36

A **clause** in a listing agreement refers to an accord a property owner makes with a real estate broker, saying the owner will pay the broker to lease or sell the property for a given price. An automatic extension makes the listing agreement persist after it expires, for a specified time.

Which of the following is true for the automatic extensions of time on listing agreements?

A) A good business practice
B) It is illegal
C) Unethical
D) None of the above

37

Appraisal refers to the assessment of real property. Which of the following kinds of appraisal do retail purchasers most likely to rely on?

A) Cost Approach
B) Reconciliation of Value Approach
C) Income Approach
D) Comparative Sales Approach

38

Section 1031, a section of the U.S. Internal Revenue Service Code, allows investors to defer capital gains taxes on any exchange of this kind of properties for business or investment purposes.

Which of the following is the term that describes the properties involved in a 1031 exchange?

A) Vacant properties
B) Transitional properties
C) Community-owned properties
D) Like-kind properties

39

Dave wants to buy a real estate wherein he can expect a cap rate of 12%.

Which of the following is the price of the real estate, given that the net operating income is $7,800 per year?

A) $65,000
B) $78,000
C) $81,250
D) $93,600

CONTINUE ▶

40

A buyer purchases a home for $4,500,000. He acquired a 30-year loan at 6.5% interest with a 20% down payment.

Which of the following is the amount of interest that the buyer needs to pay over the life of the loan?

A) $2,134,925
B) $4,677,984
C) $4,591,584
D) $4,321,125

41

A **prudent investment** is using the financial assets suitable for the risk and return profile and the time horizon of a given investor. Fiduciaries (such as financial advisors, CPAs, and others) entrusted with making prudent investments should ensure that an investment should make sense within the investor's overall portfolio and its fees should not detract significantly from the investment's returns. A good fiduciary should monitor the performance of the investments he has chosen for his clients, making sure that they are achieving their stated goals.

Which of the following should not be a prudent investment of a first time investor?

A) Six-family residential building
B) Vacant land
C) Thirty-unit suburban motel
D) Five-unit strip shopping center

42

A property originally purchased a year ago for $1,750,000 is now valued at $1,915,000. What is the percentage rate of appreciation?

A) 4.5%
B) 8.6%
C) 9.4%
D) 91%

43

Jones v. Alfred H. Mayer Co., 392 U.S. 409 (1968), is a landmark United States Supreme Court case, which held that Congress could regulate the sale of private property to prevent racial discrimination.

Which of the following provisions does the Jones v. Mayer Decision uphold?

A) Article 12A
B) Civil Rights Act of 1866
C) Federal Fair Housing Act of 1968
D) New York State Executive Law

CONTINUE ▶

The Capitalization Rate, usually called **Cap Rate**, is computed based on the ratio of the Net Operating Income (NOI) of a property to its asset value. So, for example, if a property was listed for $1,000,000 and generated an NOI of $100,000, then the cap rate would be $100,000/$1,000,000, or 10%.

Zion bought a rental property for $151,000. The property has a revenue of $18,000 a year and net operating expenses of $4,000 each year.

Which of the following is the property's cap rate?

A) 11.92%
B) 9.27%
C) 6.27%
D) 2.65%

SECTION 5

#	Answer	Topic	Subtopic	#	Answer	Topic	Subtopic	#	Answer	Topic	Subtopic	#	Answer	Topic	Subtopic
1	D	TD	SD2	12	D	TA	SA6	23	D	TA	SA2	34	D	TD	SD1
2	A	TA	SA4	13	C	TD	SD2	24	A	TA	SA1	35	A	TA	SA7
3	C	TB	SB1	14	B	TA	SA4	25	A	TB	SB1	36	B	TA	SA7
4	D	TA	SA3	15	A	TD	SD2	26	A	TD	SD5	37	D	TA	SA1
5	B	TD	SD7	16	D	TD	SD5	27	A	TB	SB1	38	D	TD	SD2
6	B	TD	SD4	17	B	TD	SD6	28	A	TA	SA4	39	A	TA	SA3
7	B	TD	SD4	18	D	TA	SA2	29	C	TD	SD7	40	C	TA	SA2
8	A	TD	SD1	19	D	TD	SD4	30	C	TB	SB3	41	B	TA	SA1
9	A	TD	SD2	20	B	TD	SD4	31	B	TA	SA3	42	C	TA	SA1
10	A	TD	SD2	21	C	TA	SA3	32	C	TD	SD5	43	B	TB	SB2
11	A	TD	SD2	22	C	TB	SB4	33	B	TA	SA4	44	B	TA	SA3

Topics & Subtopics

Code	Description	Code	Description
SA1	Commercial Investment	SD1	Construction & Environmental Issues
SA2	Estates & Interests	SD2	Deeds & Title Closing Costs
SA3	Income Approach to Real Estate Valuation	SD4	Real Estate Investment & Analysis
SA4	Mortgage Brokerage	SD5	The contract of sales and leases
SA6	Real Estate Math	SD6	Valuation
SA7	Real Estate Market	SD7	Forms of Property Ownership
SB1	Condominiums & Suites	TA	Economics
SB2	Human Rights & Fair Housing	TB	Rules & Regulations
SB3	Land Use & Regulations	TD	Transactions & Processes
SB4	Law of Agency		

TEST DIRECTION

DIRECTIONS

Read the questions carefully and then choose the ONE best answer to each question.

Be sure to allocate your time carefully so you are able to complete the entire test within the testing session. You may go back and review your answers at any time.

You may use any available space in your test booklet for scratch work.

Questions in this booklet are not actual test questions but they are the samples for commonly asked questions.

This test aims to cover all topics which may appear on the actual test. However some topics may not be covered.

Studying this booklet will be preparing you for the actual test. It will not guarantee improving your test score but it will help you pass your exam on the first attempt.

Some useful tips for answering multiple choice questions;

- Start with the questions that you can easily answer.

- Underline the keywords in the question.

- Be sure to read all the choices given.

- Watch for keywords such as NOT, always, only, all, never, completely.

- Do not forget to answer every question.

1

Which of the following is the phenomenon of owing more at the end of the year than at the beginning?

A) Deficiency
B) Negative amortization
C) Wrap around mortgage
D) Usury

2

An **automatic renewal clause,** also called as self-renewal or evergreen clause, acts to renew a contract if notice to terminate perpetually is not provided within a generally specific and relatively small window of time (for example, 30 days before the end of the term).

Which of the following refers to an automatic renewal clause in a lease?

A) It is illegal
B) It is good for the tenant
C) It is good for the landlord
D) It is good for the landlord and the tenant

3

British Thermal Unit (BTU) is part of the British Imperial system of units.

Which of the following does the British Thermal Unit measure?

A) Skill
B) Energy
C) Electricity
D) None of the above

4

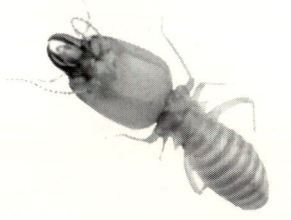

Termite is an insect living in large colonies with different castes, typically in a mound of cemented earth.

Which of the following may stop termites?

A) DDT
B) PCBs
C) Chlordane
D) None of the above

5

Which of the following is termed for a legal description written regarding angles and distances?

A) Plat of Lots
B) Lot and Block
C) Metes and Bounds
D) None of the above

6

Which of the following describes alienation?

A) To transfer real property from one person to another
B) The legal process involved in obtaining an easement by prescription
C) To acquire property in an open, hostile, and continuous manner over time
D) To acquire alluvion through a court proceeding

7

Which of the following describes a tenancy by the entirety?

A) Equal or unequal undivided ownership between two or more people
B) Ownership that's available for Limited Liabilities
C) Ownership which requires the four unities: Interest, Possession, Time, and Title
D) Ownership that is available only to married couples, tenancy by the entirety means that property may not be sold without the agreement of both parties.

8

Which of the following is the maximum age for a real estate salesperson/broker?

A) 20
B) 24
C) 65
D) None of the above

CONTINUE ▶

9

Which of the following refers to an appraisal process which uses comparisons of similar properties in the same neighborhood?

A) Cost Approach
B) Pricing Method
C) Market Data Approach
D) All of the above

10

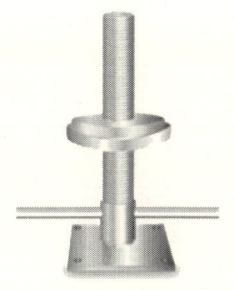

Lally Column is a tubular steel column filled with concrete. It is used as a supporting member in a building.

Where are these normally found?

A) Attic
B) Basement
C) Bathrooms
D) Closets

11

A **short sale** is where the net proceeds from selling the property will fall short of the debts secured by liens against the property.

Which of the following refers to the outstanding balance owed on a loan after the property has been sold at a short sale?

A) Arrears
B) Deficit
C) Deficiency
D) None of the answers are correct.

12

Restriction is an official rule which limits what you can do.

Which of the following estates has the fewest restrictions on the holder of it?

A) Legal title
B) Absolute life estate
C) Fee simple absolute
D) Fee simple determinable

13

Which of the following is determined by a real estate agent when gathering data for a seller?

A) A reasonable asking price for the property on the market
B) The value a lender will place on the property when it is purchased
C) The exact value of the property on that particular date
D) None of the above

14

Marty and Belle hold a piece of property as joint tenants. Marty decides to sell his interest to Clint.

How do Belle and Clint hold their interest?

A) Joint and several tenants
B) Tenants in common
C) Tenants by the entirety
D) There are insufficient facts to make this determination.

15

Building foundation supports a building from underneath.

Which of the following is the material that is most commonly used for foundations?

A) Concrete
B) Steel
C) PVC
D) Wood

16

Milly woke up one morning after a violent storm and discovered that a large chunk of her riverbank vanished.

In which of the following does this situation fall?

A) Attrition
B) Dissipation
C) Reliction
D) None of the answers are correct.

17

"Time is of the Essence" is used as a phrase in a contract referring to the performance by a party at or within the period specified in the contract. Failure to perform within the required time constitutes a breIt drops from the contractach in the contract.

Which of the following happens to the closing date when "time is of the essence" is invoked?

A) It drops from the contract
B) It loses its importance
C) It becomes significant
D) None of the above

18

Which of the following choices describes the legal method of decreasing an investor's taxable income?

A) Insurance claim
B) Return on investment
C) Tax shelter
D) Vacancy loss

19

Source of income refers to where your money is coming from. An individual income can be from multiple sources such as employment, investment and welfare. On the other hand business income can be from particular markets, products, customers, investments or government grants.

Which of the following is a source of income other than rent?

A) Laundromats
B) Mortgage interest
C) Property taxes
D) Vacancy

20

Which of the following refers to the process where there is an increase in real property by nature such as the buildup of silt?

A) Accretion
B) Addition
C) Erosion
D) Probate

21

Peter wants to sell his three-bedroom house for $250,000, but all other similar homes in the area are selling for $225,000 each.

Which of the following principles tells that Peter's home is more likely to be worth $225,000?

A) Contribution
B) Balance
C) Substitution
D) Supply

22

The **cost approach** refers to a real estate valuation method which surmises that the price a buyer should pay for a piece of property should be equal to the cost to build an equivalent building.

In which of the following circumstances would a cost approach be most useful?

A) A retail buyer who is looking for a home he plans to stay in for many years
B) An investor who wants to maximize his profit margin from renting out a property
C) A new construction property in an area with nearby available land
D) All of these answers are equally appropriate

23

On a closing statement dated May 15th, how would a $1,600/month tenant's prepaid rent appear?

A) Debit buyer $800
B) Debit seller $800
C) Debit buyer $800, Credit seller $800
D) Debit seller $800, Credit buyer $800

24

The U.S. Government describes **lead-based paint** as a paint or coating containing lead in 0.5% by weight or equal to or greater than one milligram per square centimeter.

Which of the following statements is true?

A) The presence of lead paint in homes must always be disclosed.
B) The presence of lead paint in homes must never be disclosed if the home is being purchased using an FHA loan.
C) The presence of lead paint in homes must never be disclosed.
D) None of the above

CONTINUE ▶

25

Obtaining a mortgage is an essential part of the buying process, while securing mortgage pre-qualification and pre-approval are necessary steps, assuring lenders that you'll be able to afford payments.

Which of the following can a pre-approval letter substitute?

A) Agent qualifying
B) State disclosure form
C) Mortgage commitment
D) Lead-based paint disclosure

26

Urea-formaldehyde foam insulation (UFFI) was used extensively in the 1970s. Homeowners used UFFI as a wall cavity filler at the time to conserve energy. Then, it was injected inside the walls and the final product acted as an insulating agent.

Which of the following is the advantage of urea formaldehyde foam insulation over other insulations?

A) It is contaminant-free
B) It is easy to install
C) It is less expensive
D) None of the above

27

A **contract clause** refers to a specific section within a written contract which defines the duties, rights, and privileges that each party has under the contract terms

Which of the following describes a contract clause that will allow either party to void the contract if a certain condition occurs?

A) Cogency
B) Contingency
C) Deficiency
D) Disciple

CONTINUE ▶

28

A **septic tank** refers to a watertight chamber which is usually made of concrete, fiberglass or PVC through which domestic wastewater flows for primary treatment.

Which of the following is the percentage of American homes having septic systems?

A) 25%
B) 15%
C) 10%
D) 5%

29

Comparables (also know as comps) is a real estate appraisal term that refers to different properties with similar characteristics to a subject property whose value is being sought.

Which of the following is the minimum of comps required mostly by secondary lenders to ensure an accurate estimation of a value when performing the sales comparison approach?

A) 5
B) 4
C) 3
D) 2

30

Undivided loyalty prohibits an agent from getting any advance interests adverse to her client or conducting her client's business to benefit herself or others.

Which of the following is considered in undivided loyalty?

A) Agent
B) Broker
C) Client
D) Customer

31

Lead-contaminated dust is one of the most common causes of **leadpoisoning**. The federal government banned the uses of lead-containing paints, but some states banned it even earlier.

When did federal lead-based paint disclosure laws go into effect?

A) 1995
B) 1977
C) 1996
D) 1994

32

Anne has a future interest in a house, but she only is entitled to possession of the house if Don stops using it as a residence.

What type of future interest does Anne have?

A) Her interest is vested.
B) Her interest is contingent.
C) She doesn't have a future interest.
D) She has a future possessory interest.

33

Mortgage refers to a loan which is secured by property or real estate. In exchange for funds received by the homebuyer to buy property or a home, a lender gets the promise of that buyer to pay back the funds within a specific time frame for a particular cost.

Which of the following makes home mortgages available to the public?

A) Credit unions
B) Mortgage bankers
C) Savings banks
D) All of the above

34

Two almost identical houses are located in an A+ rated school district and a mediocre school district, respectively. Because of this, the house in the A+ school district is likely to sell for more money.

Which of the following types of consideration does this indicate?

A) Economic
B) Government
C) Physical
D) Social

35

According to which of the following is the remaining fuel in a storage tank at closing apportioned and paid for?

A) Current market value
B) The average price of the time the seller purchased it
C) The purchase price of the seller
D) None of the above

36

A **title** refers to proof of ownership on a property.

In which of the following is the least assurance of title offered?

A) A Trust Deed
B) A Full Warranty Deed
C) A Bargain and Sale deed with covenants
D) A Bargain and Sale deed without covenants

38

You are trying to price a property. Five years ago, it was sold for $1,450,000, but property values in this particular neighborhood have decreased by an average of 5% since then.

Which of the following is the rough value of this property?

A) $1,400,000
B) $1,377,500
C) $1,300,000
D) $825,000

39

A commission of $13,200 was received by a broker for selling a property priced at $240,000.

What was the broker's commission rate?

A) 5.0%
B) 5.5%
C) 6.0%
D) 6.5%

40

Ownership of mineral rights refers to an estate in real property which is the right of the owner to exploit, mine, or produce any or all of the minerals lying below the surface of the property.

Which of the following can an owner of both surface and mineral estate do?

A) Sell the mineral rights.
B) Lease the mineral rights.
C) Sell the surface estate but keep the mineral rights.
D) All of the above

41

The **trustee** manages or holds assets, cash or a property title.

Which of the following benefits when the trustee is held in a property?

A) Beneficiary
B) Grantor
C) Heir
D) Decedent

42

Section 1031 is under the section of the U.S. Internal Revenue Service Code tackling any exchange of properties for business or investment purposes.

Which of the following is the primary purpose of a 1031 exchange?

A) Transfer owned property to a family member before the owner's death without paying taxes.
B) Transfer the property to a non-family member upon the owner's death.
C) Delay paying taxes when selling one rental investment and using the funds to purchase a similar income producing property.
D) None of these answers are correct.

43

Which of the following refers to the situation called **Pro-ration** during a corporate action in which the available cash or shares are not sufficient to satisfy the offers tendered by shareholders?

A) The process of settling a will
B) The process of the government taking an individual's land under eminent domain
C) The time necessary for a variance to hold before the planning board
D) The apportionment of expenses and assets of buyer and seller at closing

Multifamily residential refers to a type of housing where several separate residential units are within one building or several buildings within one complex.

Which of the following is a disadvantage of owning a multi-family housing?

A) Owners may receive multiple rent checks each month.
B) A vacancy in one unit would not eliminate income flow from the property.
C) The owner may be able to avoid commercial financing if he or she lives in one of the units.
D) Generally, there are less potential buyers for units in multi-family properties.

SECTION 6

#	Answer	Topic	Subtopic	#	Answer	Topic	Subtopic	#	Answer	Topic	Subtopic	#	Answer	Topic	Subtopic
1	B	TA	SA5	12	C	TD	SD7	23	D	TD	SD2	34	D	TA	SA7
2	A	TD	SD5	13	A	TD	SD4	24	A	TD	SD1	35	A	TD	SD2
3	B	TD	SD1	14	B	TD	SD7	25	A	TA	SA5	36	D	TD	SD2
4	D	TD	SD1	15	A	TD	SD1	26	D	TD	SD1	37	A	TD	SD7
5	C	TD	SD2	16	D	TD	SD7	27	B	TD	SD5	38	B	TA	SA2
6	A	TD	SD2	17	C	TD	SD5	28	C	TD	SD1	39	B	TA	SA6
7	D	TD	SD2	18	C	TA	SA6	29	C	TA	SA4	40	D	TD	SD7
8	D	TA	SA7	19	A	TA	SA3	30	C	TA	SA1	41	A	TA	SA2
9	C	TD	SD6	20	A	TD	SD2	31	C	TD	SD1	42	C	TD	SD4
10	B	TD	SD1	21	C	TA	SA7	32	B	TD	SD7	43	D	TD	SD2
11	C	TD	SD7	22	C	TA	SA7	33	D	TA	SA5	44	D	TD	SD4

Topics & Subtopics

Code	Description	Code	Description
SA1	Commercial Investment	SD2	Deeds & Title Closing Costs
SA2	Estates & Interests	SD4	Real Estate Investment & Analysis
SA3	Income Approach to Real Estate Valuation	SD5	The contract of sales and leases
SA4	Mortgage Brokerage	SD6	Valuation
SA5	Real Estate Finance	SD7	Forms of Property Ownership
SA6	Real Estate Math	TA	Economics
SA7	Real Estate Market	TD	Transactions & Processes
SD1	Construction & Environmental Issues		

Made in United States
North Haven, CT
08 May 2023